I0492470

The On-Camera Confidence Handbook

Eleven Easy Steps to Beat Camera Shyness and Take Your Brand to the World, Even with Just Your Smartphone

(A Lights, Camera, Action Planner)

By Rob Deptford

The On-Camera Confidence Handbook

Copyright © 2022 Robert Deptford

E-mail: eq4media@gmail.com

www.getoncamera.com

ISBN - 9798685397928

Printed in the United States of America

The Struggle with Camera Shyness

Fear of the camera is common. We've all been to gatherings where someone tries to capture the memories in snapshots or on video, and certain people hide out in another room hoping to avoid the impromptu photography session.

For those who are not camera shy, such fear seems incomprehensible. After all, what harm can a little black hand-held device possibly do?

But those who are camera shy know the psychological trauma all too well. Some are even quite comfortable presenting to colleagues at the office or speaking to large audiences on stage, but put them in front of a camera, and they completely freeze up.

What causes such seemingly irrational behaviour? I'm not a psychology expert, but in my experience, it's usually one of two things.

The first is technophobia. Some of us remember having cell phones the size of a brick. And we used them to talk to other people!

The latest smartphones have replaced our newspapers, books, wallets, notepads, calendars, music players, cameras and more. That much functionality takes time to learn and the haphazardness of a child to simply push buttons and watch what happens.

The On-Camera Confidence Handbook

I assure you, pressing the video recording button on your smartphone will not cause it to malfunction in any way!

The second and more common reason I see for camera shyness is a fear of how we might look or sound on video. When we're self-conscious, it's easy to worry about how other people might judge us, especially when we have preconceived ideas about the kinds of people who are truly photogenic and have voices anyone would enjoy listening to.

Without such fears and nervousness, we wouldn't know we were at our boundaries, and that we have an opportunity to overcome them by learning something new.

A perspective shift changes the game when we're feeling anxious about going on camera, or anything else for that matter.

When we learn to interpret fear as a sign of opportunity, we can also interpret nervousness as excitement, and it just gets easier to do when we see the results of our courage.

I used to be camera shy. Going to broadcasting school helped me face my fear and become more comfortable in my own skin. Knowing I wanted to reap the benefits of that hard work for my career motivated me to make it happen.

You don't have to go to broadcasting school to learn video, but you do have to decide to face your fear. Since you're reading this, I trust you've made that decision for the benefit of your business. Get excited and have some fun with it!

Step 1: Step into Star Power

I'm an introvert. I prefer small social circles, quiet environments and lots of time alone with my own thoughts.

And yet, I've made a career out of leveraging skills often assumed to be the expertise of extroverts – speaking to thousands of people beginning in broadcast journalism and meandering through roles that required on-stage presentation skills and a dynamic presence that made audiences feel as though they should be listening closely to what I had to say.

How is this possible? I discovered that with motivation to succeed and some effort, I could stretch out of my comfort zone and step into my star power.

Sure, I had the benefit of broadcast training, but I had to choose that course of study. That simply shows these unique communication skills and strategies are learnable if you want to learn them.

And you should want to learn them.

Even before the global pandemic of 2020, consumers were increasingly looking for online video from brands to help them make buying decisions, and now that transformation has been catalyzed.

Your audience is waiting in the digital realm for you to step into your star power on camera and give them reasons to do business with you. Here comes the first of your action steps.

And... Action!

List five people you know have star power, and that you admire. Why do you admire them? Note the specific characteristics you appreciate. Which attributes might you want to develop for yourself?

Star 1:

Characteristics I like:

Attributes I'd like to develop:

Star 2:

Characteristics I like:

Attributes I'd like to develop:

Star 3:

Characteristics I like:

Attributes I'd like to develop:

Star 4:

Characteristics I like:

Attributes I'd like to develop:

Star 5:

Characteristics I like:

Attributes I'd like to develop:

Step 2: Find Your Motivation

As the world transforms in the digital-first business era, what do you want for your business and from your business?

It's probably a safe bet that, at the very least, you want your business to survive and generate enough revenue to pay your bills.

But what are the bigger things you want – the things you dream about?

Even more importantly, why are those things meaningful to you?

These are not always easy questions to answer, particularly during times of adaptation forced by circumstances beyond your control. That said, once you do come up with some clear, concise answers, you will undoubtedly discover what motivates you.

Those goals and dreams – those motivators – are the keys to getting past fears and forging ahead in new ways, including getting in front of a camera as part of your digital marketing evolution.

Pressing the record button can be a big hurdle to clear, but when you know there is the potential for highly valued rewards as a result of your courage, fear gets a lot easier to manage.

And... Action!

List five things you truly want that will motivate you to learn video, and perhaps other new business tools. They could be anything from more sales leads to more vacation time to opportunities help others.

Then list why these things are meaningful to you.

1. I want...

This is why it is meaningful to me:

2. I want…

This is why it is meaningful to me:

3. I want…

This is why it is meaningful to me:

4. I want…

This is why it is meaningful to me:

5. I want…

This is why it is meaningful to me:

Step 3: Eat, Sleep and Be Merry

Recording a message on camera is a performance, and it requires you to take control of factors you know have an impact on how you show up.

Choose to eat right. Fruit, vegetables, whole grains and lean meats are best.

Avoid dairy products before a recording as they can increase mucus and effect vocal quality. Also, avoid energy draining fatty and fast foods as well as alcohol, which can dry out vocal cords and inhibit performance.

Caffeine is a known performance enhancer, but use it sparingly before recording as it can dehydrate you.

Another performance enhancer is regular exercise. Cardiovascular and core strengthening activities are particularly helpful for speakers as they increase lung capacity and improve vocal projection.

Finally, getting enough sleep is critical to delivering your best performance. Sleeping is often criticized, as though it's a status symbol to be able to get by on very little sleep, but the reality is that healthy adults need seven to nine hours of sleep for proper body function.

When your body feels good your mood improves, and you feel more confident in any situation, including being in front of the camera.

And... Action!

Diet, exercise and sleep habits are not easy to change. That's why there are multi-billion-dollar industries built around helping people make such changes.

Consider taking just a small, manageable step by noting your current habits for a week. Pay attention to how you feel, then evaluate what you might like to change.

Day 1:

Breakfast:

Lunch:

Dinner:

Snacks:

Exercise completed:

Hours of sleep:

The On-Camera Confidence Handbook

Day 2:

Breakfast:

Lunch:

Dinner:

Snacks:

Exercise completed:

Hours of sleep:

The On-Camera Confidence Handbook

Day 3:

Breakfast:

Lunch:

Dinner:

Snacks:

Exercise completed:

Hours of sleep:

Day 4:

Breakfast:

Lunch:

Dinner:

Snacks:

Exercise completed:

Hours of sleep:

Day 5:

Breakfast:

Lunch:

Dinner:

Snacks:

Exercise completed:

Hours of sleep:

Day 6:

Breakfast:

Lunch:

Dinner:

Snacks:

Exercise completed:

Hours of sleep:

Day 7:

Breakfast:

Lunch:

Dinner:

Snacks:

Exercise completed:

Hours of sleep:

Step 4: Choose a Productive Time

My wife and I are morning people. We wake up most days at 5:30 a.m., and my wife leaves for work by 7:00 a.m. I exercise, eat, take my kids to school, and then start my work day by 9:00 a.m.

I've come to learn that if I need to perform on camera, or if I have anything challenging to accomplish, I need to attack it before noon for best results. At around 2:00 p.m. I start to fade, and while sometimes an afternoon cup of coffee will boost my spirits for a couple more hours, I don't normally have the cognitive power for any serious work in the late afternoon.

Sometimes my brain decides to generate ideas in the late evening, but usually I'm quickly asleep when I go to bed around 10:00 p.m., and that allows for a healthy amount of sleep most nights.

By contrast, I know people who scoff at the idea of going to bed at such an early hour, and they would never voluntarily start their day before the sun rises.

These so-called night owls are often most productive during the evening, or even the wee hours of the morning when we morning people are sound asleep.

So, for beginner video creators (and experts who still get a little nervous), why not plan to do your recording at whatever part of the day is your peak time?

And... Action!

Once you're aware of the time(s) of day you're at your best, consider a time management system such as this blocking chart to plan your video creation at your peak times.

	Mon	Tues	Wed	Thurs	Fri
6am	Breakfast	Breakfast	Breakfast	Breakfast	Breakfast
7am	Exercise	Exercise	Exercise	Exercise	Exercise
8am	Take kids to school	Take kids to school	Take kids to school	Take kids to school	Take kids to school
9am **PEAK**		Teach video mastermind	Video location scouting	Teach video mastermind	Write video script
10am **PEAK**	Record podcast episode	Write video script		Record video	Record video
11am **PEAK**	Conduct webinar	Record video	Conduct webinar	Record video	Conduct webinar
12pm	Lunch	Lunch	Lunch	Lunch	Lunch

1pm	Client video calls	Client video calls	Client video calls	Client video calls	Client video calls
2pm	Social media engagement	Social media engagement	Social media engagement	Social media engagement	Social media engagement
3pm	Pick up kids from school	Pick up kids from school	Pick up kids from school	Pick up kids from school	Pick up kids from school
4pm	Kids hockey practice	Overseas client video calls	Publication writing	Overseas client video calls	Meet friends at pub
5pm		Kids hockey practice		Kids hockey practice	
6pm			Hockey game		
7pm					
8pm					
9pm	Review, reflect and plan	Review, reflect and plan	Review, reflect and plan	Review, reflect and plan	Review, reflect and plan
10pm	Bed time	Bed time	Bed time	Bed time	Bed time

Step 5: Dress the Part

Clothes make a difference. A quick online search will show you lots of different science behind why what we wear matters, but we really don't have to dig very deep to know it's true.

Consider, for example, how comfortable and at ease you feel in your favourite pair of jeans, or how awkward you feel in something that just isn't your style.

Granted, there's a level of practicality to consider. You probably wouldn't wear your cowboy hat and boots to speak to a group of opera fans. Or, maybe you're rebellious like that.

The point is that there is a sweet spot between what you like to wear and what will give you an appearance acceptable to your audience.

When you find that sweet spot, stick with it, and think of it as a mechanism for getting into character for your recording, just like actors do.

As a bonus, your personal brand will benefit. Think back to the first exercise where you listed several people who have star power. How do they dress? Chances are, they have a signature outfit or accessory they have become known for, and that you expect to see.

Your audience will eventually expect to see your personal brand appearance, too.

And... Action!

Take stock of what's in your closet that might be appropriate for your on-camera appearance, and prepare to invest in some new pieces. Follow this checklist:

1. Do you like it?
   - o YES
   - o NO
2. Does it fit properly?
   - o YES
   - o NO
3. Is it reflective of how you want to be known?
   - o YES
   - o NO
4. Does it make you feel empowered?
   - o YES
   - o NO
5. Is it repeatable? (You can comfortably wear it regularly.)
   - o YES
   - o NO

You've got a winner if you check YES for all five!

Tech tip: Avoid busy patterns. Cameras do best with solid, neutral colours, especially if you're a novice videographer using minimal equipment.

Step 6: Write Your Talking Points

If you have ever had to give a speech, you know it's not easy for most people. After all, we don't typically do it every day.

Like camera shyness, stage fright is extremely common. And while you may have heard all the usual tips from deep breathing to picturing the audience in their underwear, there isn't anything more effective than being well prepared.

The good news with video recording is that there is no audience. At least, there's no audience in the room with you.

As well, it doesn't matter if you mess up. You can record again and again – a hundred times if necessary – until you're happy with the outcome.

Let's face it, though – most of us need to be efficient because we have other things to do during our business day.

That's why you should write down your talking points and go through them a few times before you start recording.

I'm not suggesting you write an entire script word for word at this point, although there is a time and place for that. For the purpose of gaining confidence, just pick two or three simple talking points you can cover in a minute or less.

By writing things down in bite-sized pieces, you'll have an easier time memorizing and delivering your message.

And... Action!

Time goes by faster than you may realize when you're speaking on camera. If you're nervous, you may speak more quickly. It's common to then overcorrect and speak too slowly.

Try writing talking points in the following three-part format. Speak for about 20 seconds per segment, and adjust until you feel you are speaking at a comfortable conversational pace within the time limit.

Tech tip: Use a timer to help stay on pace.

Talking points:

1. (20 seconds)

    Quick intro point:

    Segue:

2. (20 seconds)

    Main point:

    Segue:

3. (20 seconds)

   Final point:

   Wrap-up:

Step 7: Reflection. Literally.

Sometimes we just have to take a look in the mirror, and in this case, that's exactly what we should do.

Once we're aware of how we want to present ourselves, and we're motivated, in the right mood, and in the right clothes at the right time, the next part is rehearsal.

You may not know exactly how you appear to others, especially if you have little to no experience with feedback on presentations or public speaking.

It's amazing what little distracting habits we form when we're in circumstances that make us uncomfortable. You have probably noticed some of those distracting behaviours when watching others on stage, television, or online. They range from lack of eye contact to hair flipping to fidgeting with pens or electronic devices.

A common saying is that the camera adds 10 pounds, but that's not exactly true. Cameras are simply very good at magnifying things for the audience. As such, every movement you make, intentional or not, becomes much more noticeable on a video recording.

Practice is the solution. It pays to rehearse what you want to say while paying close attention to your body language. And if you're not yet ready to be critiqued by someone else, standing in front of a mirror is a great place to start.

And... Action!

Plan a dress rehearsal in front of the mirror. Bring along your talking points, timer, a glass of water and anything else that might help you feel comfortable.

Practice going through your talking points several times and carefully observe your delivery.

What are your eyes doing? What are your hands doing? How is your body behaving in general? What do you want to change?

Self-Critique Notes:

Self-Critique Notes:

Self-Critique Notes:

The On-Camera Confidence Handbook

Self-Critique Notes:

Self-Critique Notes:

Self-Critique Notes:

Step 8: Record for Your Eyes Only

This is it! It's time to get in front of your camera, smartphone or webcam and press the record button.

Are your knees trembling at the thought?

As mentioned earlier, most people worry about how they will look on screen, how they will sound when they speak, and how other people might judge their performance.

These are all valid concerns because – let's face it – you're probably not a professional broadcaster or a famous movies star. The key is to be okay with that, and to be okay with being yourself.

After all, what makes famous broadcasters, singers, actors and other performers so appealing to their audience?

Talent? Sure.

But what really makes the difference for performers who get noticed is their uniqueness and authenticity.

And guess what? People judge those famous performers. Just follow the Twitter account of anyone in the public eye, and you'll see a myriad of both positive and negative comments.

We just have to decide not to care what people think, because the right people will think the right things.

Making that decision will take a huge weight off.

And... Action!

Just like you did in front of the mirror, plan a dress rehearsal in front of the camera.

The difference this time is that you won't be able to see your delivery as you're speaking, so think about what you observed in front of the mirror, and be conscious of how you want to show up.

Practice several times in a row without stopping the recording, then sit down, relax, play it back and do a self-critique.

Self-Critique Notes:

The On-Camera Confidence Handbook

Self-Critique Notes:

Self-Critique Notes:

Self-Critique Notes:

Self-Critique Notes:

Self-Critique Notes:

Step 9: Consult Someone You Trust

You're getting closer to being a confident on-camera spokesperson for your business!

All the practice you've done up to this point should have eased some of your anxiety, but even if it hasn't, there's nothing like the support of a close friend or family member to help break through barriers.

The next step is to join someone in your comfort zone, and whose honest opinion you value, for drinks, coffee, lunch, or whatever your typical conversational social activity might be.

When you're deciding who to invite, consider who you might ask for good, unbiased judgement about what you're wearing, the style of furniture you're thinking about buying, etc. (See, we even invite others to judge us sometimes!)

Let them know you're on an exciting journey to learn a new business skill and that you would appreciate hearing their comments and suggestions on how to improve.

Take your phone with some of your favourite self-recordings – and even some of your not-so-favourite ones – loaded and ready to share. We tend to be hard on ourselves, and some of those recordings you thought were trash may be stellar from the perspective of someone else.

At the pub, restaurant or coffee shop, you're buying.

And... Action!

This is your first feedback from someone else, and it is your first indicator of how your audience may react to your on-camera performance. It really counts. Take notes and carefully consider all comments and suggestions.

Better yet, make sure your trusted critique partner has access to your recordings for a few days so they can be more carefully reviewed. Then have them send you their comments.

Critique Partner Notes:

Critique Partner Notes:

Critique Partner Notes:

Critique Partner Notes:

Critique Partner Notes:

Critique Partner Notes:

Step 10: Publish

Now comes the real test. You have prepared, practiced and analyzed your on-camera speaking skills, and you have had someone else give their analysis of your efforts.

But sadly, analysis paralysis is all too real, and this is where many people stall.

If you are still truly mindful of your business goals and how you want to leverage the necessary video marketing and communication tools to help you reach those goals in the digital-first business era, this is where you have to decide to take a leap of faith.

It's time to publish your first video.

Where should you do that? I recommend posting on a social media platform with few video restrictions, like Facebook or LinkedIn.

No editing required right now. Keep it raw and simple.

Consider strategies to boost your organic reach so more people will see your post. Using relevant hashtags (#video, #socialvideo, #digitalmarketing, etc.) or tagging some of your best connections so they get a notification about your post will make a difference.

Then, be sure to engage in the comments. That's where business relationships are made!

And... Action!

Write a short introductory post for your video. A good lead, a few bullet points and a call to action is all it takes for Facebook or Linkedin. If you're feeling extra creative, use relevant emojis to mark your bullet points! Check out this example:

This is my first social media video! Here's why I've decided to post video, and why you should, too...

💻 I want to become more noticeable online so I'm prepared as more consumers choose digital options

🔑 I want to communicate my value to more potential customers

🤝 I want others to get to know, like and trust me in a way that is as close to in-person interaction as possible in the digital space

How are you making digital transformations in your business? Please share in the comments.

#digitalmarketing #videomarketing #socialmedia

UPLOAD OR LINK TO VIDEO HERE

Step 11: Lather, Rinse, Repeat

You've done it! Congratulations! You broke through your barriers and posted your first video online.

Now you can breathe a sigh of relief, consider your goal achieved, and move on to the next order of business, right?

Nope.

This is just the beginning of a long-term commitment you must make to continually show up on video for your audience, and to continually interact with them.

You don't have to spend hours and hours online every day, but you do have to spend time there on a regular basis. In the same way that time blocking was shown earlier in this book as a tool to help schedule video recordings when you're at peak performance, you can also use that system to schedule regular social media time.

Try it weekly at first, or daily if you're ambitious. Either way, consistency trumps frequency.

Gone are the days of social media being a distraction from business and a waste of time. It's become the place to be for business to thrive now, and into the future.

And video is the most powerful business communication tool you can use to reach your audience there.

Bonus Tip: Basic Equipment Helps

Yes, I know the message all along has been that you can get started creating video with just your smartphone, and despite the cringing professional videographers might do, it is absolutely true. We're not setting out to create Hollywood-style movies, so we don't need Hollywood-style gear.

That said, once you're committed to creating videos on a regular basis, you will eventually want to add a few helpful items to your videography kit so you have more options to develop your creativity and improve your video quality.

The first thing to get is an external microphone. The built-in mics on smartphones have come a long way, but they're only good at very close range. As well, if you're recording outside, even a slight breeze can wash out your message with noise.

A lapel mic (also called a lavalier mic) is a tiny microphone on a clip that can be attached to your shirt or jacket somewhere between your chin and your chest, and it's a great choice for a quick and easy improvement to the sound of your recorded voice.

The second thing I recommend buying is a tripod with a smartphone clamp. You will want to stand and speak with hand expressions, so this will get your smartphone out of your hands.

Third, you should consider a light ring. We won't get into the technical aspects of lighting here, but a single light ring will improve your on-camera appearance without having to set up a whole studio in your office or home.

Fourth, get some lens cleaner and a microfiber cloth. This is the cheapest thing on the list, and if your lens is dirty, cleaning it will bring you the biggest return on investment.

Finally, a selfie stick or gimbal will round out a good starter kit.

Selfie sticks have been around for years, and they allow you to get more of your background into the image frame when you're on the go and not packing your tripod. This is important because the images you show should support the words you speak. In other words, don't just tell us a story, show us a story.

A gimbal is a supercharged selfie stick. It is battery powered and contains tiny, quiet electric motors that work together to constantly keep your shot smooth and stable. This is done through an app on your smartphone and a Bluetooth connection.

Wondering what brands to buy or where to find these things? There are many choices these days, but Amazon or your favourite electronics stores are good places to start shopping around.

I hope to see your videos in my social media feeds very soon!

More Resources

For more on media training, video marketing and business storytelling for the digital-first business era, visit:

www.stratoschool.com

To book the author for speaking engagements, email:

rob@stratoschool.com

If you found this resource valuable, please consider writing a review on Amazon.

Wishing you all the best!